Contents

Some words are shown in bold, **like this**. You can find
out what they mean by looking in the Glossary.

Where rivers begin

Rivers begin on high ground where it often rains or snows. The start of a river is called the **source**. The source of a river may be a spring.

The source of this river is high in the mountains where there is a lot of rain and snow.

TAKE-OFF!

What are ...?
RIVERS

**Andy Owen and
Miranda Ashwell**

Heinemann
LIBRARY

First published in Great Britain by Heinemann Library
Halley Court, Jordan Hill, Oxford OX2 8EJ
a division of Reed Educational and Professional Publishing Ltd.
Heinemann is a registered trademark of Reed Educational and Professional Publishing Ltd.

OXFORD MELBOURNE AUCKLAND
IBADAN JOHANNESBURG BLANTYRE GABORONE
PORTSMOUTH NH (USA) CHICAGO

Designed by Susan Clarke and Celia Floyd
Illustrations by Oxford Illustrators (maps pp.23, 25, 27)
Originated by Dot Gradations, UK
Printed in Hong Kong/China

04 03 02
10 9 8 7 6 5 4 3 2

ISBN 0 431 02340 9

British Library Cataloguing in Publication Data

Owen, Andy
  What are rivers?. – (Take off!)
  1. Rivers – Juvenile literature
  1. Title II. Ashwell, Miranda III. Rivers
  551.4'83

Acknowledgements

The Publishers would like to thank the following for permission to reproduce photographs:
Aerofilms, p.14; Air Fotos Ltd, p.15; Andy Owen, pp.7, 9; Colourific/Thomas Muscionico, p.12; Environmental Images/Graham Burns, p.19; Images Colour Library p.10; Magnum/S.T. Franklin, p.13; NRSC, pp. 22, 24, 26; Oxford Scientific Films, p.17 (Paul McCullagh), p.20 (Edward Parker); Panos Pictures/Neil Cooper, p.28; Planet Earth/Adam Jones, p.21; Still Pictures, p.29 (Andre Bartschi), p.16 (Helour Netocny), p.8 (Jim Wark); Telegraph Colour Library/Terry McCormick, p.11; Tony Stone, p.5, p.18 (Mark Lewis); Wildlife Matters, pp. 4, 6

Cover photograph: Still Pictures/Jim Wark

Our thanks to Sue Graves for her advice and expertise in the preparation of this book.

Every effort has been made to contact copyright holders of any material reproduced in this book. Any omissions will be rectified in subsequent printings if notice is given to the Publisher.

For more information about Heinemann Library books, or to order, please telephone +44(0)1865 888066, or send a fax to +44(0)1865 314091. You can visit our website at www.heinemann.co.uk

This river begins to flow as the mountain ice melts.

Some rivers start when ice melts. The ice melts in warm weather. So the river has most water in spring and summer. What do you think this river is like in the middle of winter?

Mountain rivers

Tributaries join to make a river.

Water flows down the hill in a stream. It grows into a bigger river as it is joined by other streams.

The streams that join the bigger river are called tributaries.

Water tumbles over the rocks of the **river bed** as it flows down hill. Over many years the rocks become round and smooth.

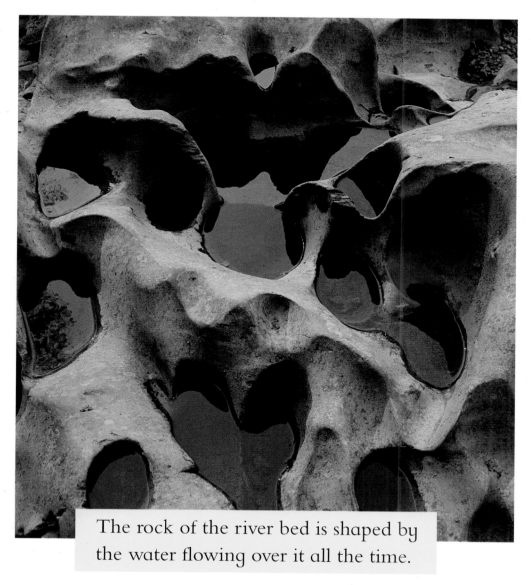

The rock of the river bed is shaped by the water flowing over it all the time.

Bends in the river

On flat land the river makes large bends or loops. These bends or loops are called **meanders**.

meander

The flowing water has made these bends and loops.

Meanders are named after the River Meander in Turkey.

Water flows quickly around the bend. On the outside of the river it **erodes** the **river bank** and makes a cliff. On the inside river bank, sand is left.

cliff

As the river flows around the meander it erodes the outside bank.

Waterfalls

Waterfalls happen when a river flows from hard rock to soft rock. The river drops over a cliff in a waterfall. The soft rock below is worn away.

hard rock cliff

The falling water makes lots of spray.

This raft is thrown about by the wild, white-water.

The river is wild and rough below the waterfall. The river flows very fast over large rocks. This part of the river is called the **rapids**. People like to go white-water rafting in rapids. White-water rafting can be a dangerous sport.

Floods

Rivers can usually cope well with rainwater. But sometimes storms are so heavy that the water spills over the **river banks** and floods the land.

Flat land by the river is the **flood plain**.

Flood water has left silt on this farmland on the flood plain.

When rivers flood they drop a rich mud, called **silt**, onto the land. Silt helps plants grow well. Flood plains make good farmland because of this silt.

Rivers meet the sea

By the time the river meets the sea it is very wide. The river flows into the sea. This is called the river **mouth**.

river mouth

The wide mouth of the river.

The river mouth can be thousands of kilometres from its **source**.

island

Large factories have been built on the flat land near the river mouth.

The river drops mud at the river mouth. This mud makes flat land next to the river. This land is called **mud flats**. The river flows around the mud flats to make little islands.

15

Using river water

Farmers take water from the river to use on their land. This is called **irrigation**. This farmer is lifting water by hand to irrigate his fields.

Using a bucket to lift water.

This farmer is using a pump to lift water from the river. The pump works very quickly so the farmer has lots of water to irrigate his land.

Using a pump to irrigate fields.

River pollution

Rubbish and chemicals from homes, factories and farms get into rivers. They make the water dirty. This is called **pollution**.

Rubbish and chemicals pollute the water.

Fish will live in the river when it is clean.

Dirty water kills fish and river plants. People try hard to get rid of river pollution. They clean the river to make it safe for fish and plants.

Work on the river

People use rivers every day in many different ways. Some people catch fish from rivers to eat or sell.

Catching fish with a net to sell at the market.

Some companies move the **products** they make by river. They have to use rivers that are deep and wide enough for big ships.

coal →

It is easier to move this coal by river.

River map 1

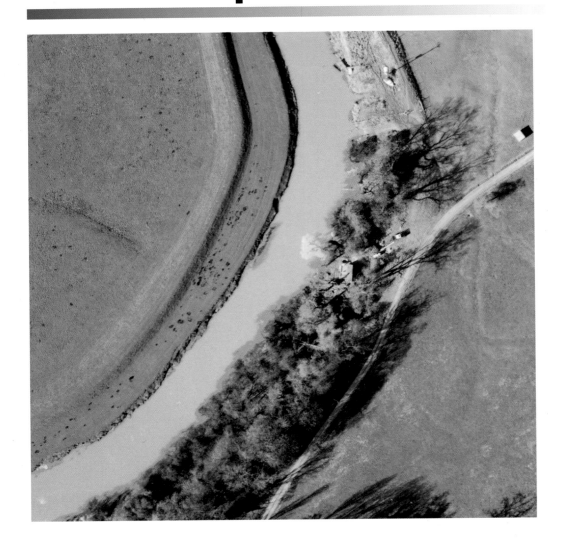

This photo was taken from an aeroplane. You can see a large bend on a river. There are fields and a wood next to the river.

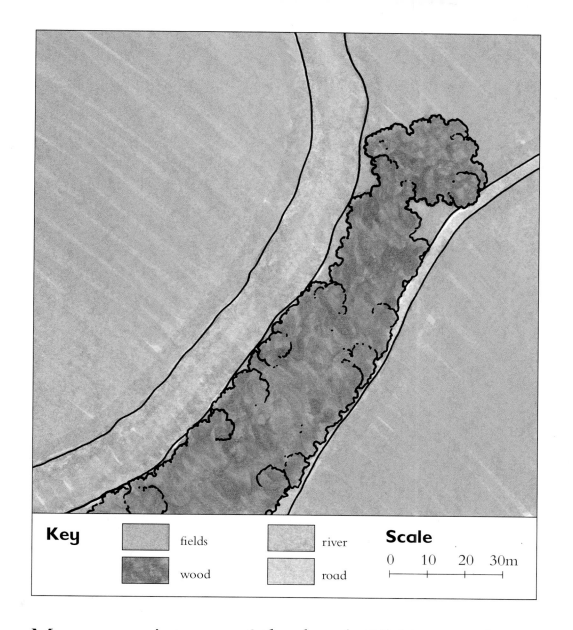

Key

▢	fields	▢	river	
▢	wood	▢	road	

Scale

0   10   20   30m

Maps are pictures of the land. This map shows us the same place as the photo. Measure the river with a piece of string. Measure the string against the scale to see how long the river is.

River map 2

farm

This photo is of the same river. The bend looks smaller but you can see more of the river. You can also see a farm.

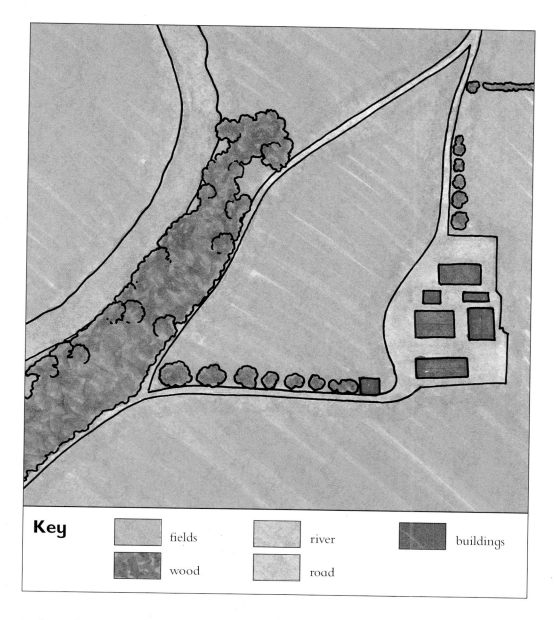

Key

fields	river	buildings
wood	road	

The key helps us to understand the map. The blue line shows the river and the grey line shows the road to the farm. Find the farm buildings, river, wood, fields and road on the map.

River map 3

bridge

In this photo you can see more of the river and more fields. There is a bridge crossing the river at the top of the photo.

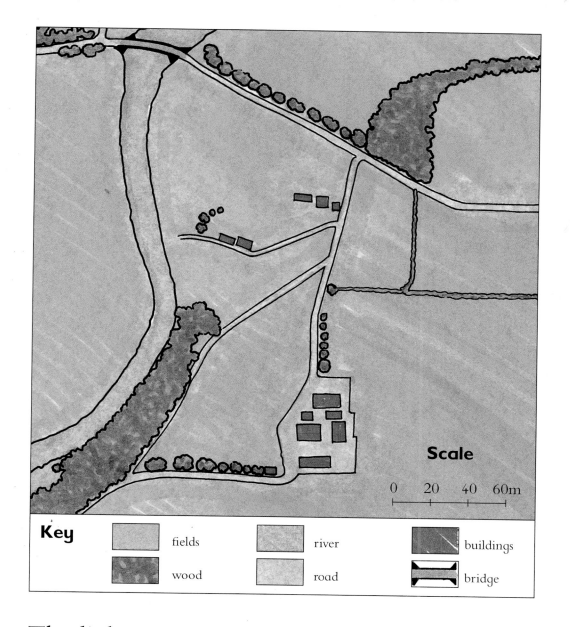

Scale

0   20   40   60m

Key

fields

wood

river

road

buildings

bridge

The light green on the map shows the fields. We can see the shape of each field. Estimate and then measure the length of the river in this map. Remember to use a piece of string to help you.

Amazing river facts

The River Amazon in South America is the biggest river. It has more water than any other river. It also flows through the biggest rainforest.

rainforest   River Amazon

The River Amazon holds one-fifth of all the river water in the world.

The River Nile in Africa is the longest river in the world. It is 6670 kilometres long. Most of the river flows through a huge desert called the Sahara Desert.

An even bigger river flows underneath the River Nile. It has six times more water that the river on top!

Glossary

erode wear away

flood plain flat land that is flooded by a river

irrigation the supply of water to land

meanders bends in a river

mouth where a river flows into the sea

mud flats flat land made of mud in or by a river

pollution dirt and rubbish in the water or air

products goods made by a factory

rapids where a river flows fast over rocks

river bank the sides of a river

river bed the bottom of a river

silt rich, fertile soil left by floodwater

source where a stream or river begins

tributaries small streams which join a river as it goes down hill

More books to read

Nicole Baxter. *Our wonderful Earth.*
Two-Can, 1997

Claire Llewellyn. *Why do we have? Rivers and Seas.*
Heinemann Library, 1997

Helena Ramsey. *Step-by-step: Rivers and Lakes.*
Franklin Watts, 1996

Carole Telford and Rod Theodorou.
Amazing Journeys: Down a River.
Heinemann Library, 1997

Index

4